thgow

baloooza readers

W9-BRY-371

EMERGING READER 2

Tweet, Oompa, Bumpety-Boom!

By Teresa Domnauer

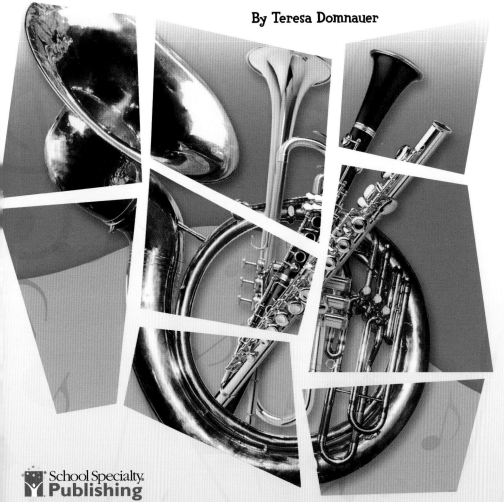

School Specialty Publishing

Text Copyright © 2006 School Specialty Publishing. Farkle McBride Character © 2000 by John Lithgow. Farkle McBride Illustration © 2000 by C.F. Payne.

Library of Congress Cataloging-in-Publication Data is on file with the publisher.

Send all inquiries to:
School Specialty Publishing
8720 Orion Place
Columbus, OH 43240-2111

ISBN 0-7696-4222-5

1 2 3 4 5 6 7 8 9 10 PHXBK 10 09 08 07 06 05

Hi, I'm Farkle McBride.
Join me in learning about
musical instruments.
Musical instruments are incredible!
Some are loud and booming.
Some have strings to strum.
All instruments do one special thing.
They make music!

Table of Contents

Guitar

What makes that
strum-strumming sound?
It is a guitar.

The guitar is part of the string family.
A player plucks the strings
with his fingers to make sound.
A guitar has a long neck
with **pegs** at the end.
Its body has a curvy shape,
just like the number 8.

Violin

What makes that
zing-zinging sound?
It is a violin.

The violin is part of the string family.
It looks like a guitar,
but it is much smaller.
A violin has four wire strings.
It is played with a **bow**
made of horsehair.
The violin makes the highest sounds
of all the stringed instruments.

Cello

What makes that
low, rolling sound?
It is a cello.

The cello looks like a big violin.
It is played with a bow.
The cello stands on the floor,
big and tall.
Its sounds are long, deep, and low.

Flute

What makes that
trill-trilling sound?
It is a flute.

A flute is a woodwind.
A woodwind makes sound
when a player blows air into it.
The flute is made of shiny metal.
It has a long, thin body
with **keys** that move.

Clarinet

What makes that
hum-humming sound?
It is a clarinet.

The clarinet is a woodwind.
It has a special **reed** made of wood.
A player blows air over the reed.
This makes sounds.
The clarinet has keys, just like a flute.
Its round bottom is the **bell**.

Bassoon

What makes that
buzz-buzzing sound?
It is a bassoon.

The big bassoon is made of wood.
Its curvy metal tube is the **crook**.
There are two little reeds
at the end of the crook.
A player blows air through the reeds.
This makes the lowest
of the woodwind sounds.

Saxophone

What makes that
sing-singing sound?
It is a saxophone.

A saxophone curves
at the top and the bottom.
It looks like the letter *S*.
The saxophone has a reed,
just like a clarinet.
It has keys, just like a flute.
Its gleaming body is made of brass.

Trumpet

What makes that
root-tooting sound?
It is a trumpet.

The trumpet is part of the brass family.
The trumpet's **mouthpiece**
looks like a little cup.
It has three **valves** on top
that look like small knobs.
A player presses the valves
to make different sounds.

Tuba

What makes that
boom-booming sound?
It is a tuba.

The tuba is the biggest brass
instrument of all.
It plays the lowest notes.
A tuba player in a marching band
carries it around her waist.
Sounds come out of its huge bell.

Snare Drum

What makes that
rat-tatting sound?
It is a snare drum.

The snare drum is part
of the percussion family.
These instruments help keep the beat.
A drummer uses drumsticks
to strike the top of the drum.
This part of the drum
is the **drumhead**.

Xylophone

What makes that
tink-tinking sound?
It is a xylophone.

The xylophone belongs to
the percussion family, too.
It is made of wooden bars.
A player uses **beaters**
to strike the bars.
This makes music that sounds
like bells.

Piano

What makes that
ping-pinging sound?
It is a piano.

The piano is a keyboard instrument.
It has 88 keys made from ivory.
The keys are attached to strings
inside the piano.
When a key is pressed, a little hammer
strikes a string.
This makes both high and low sounds.

Synthesizer

What makes all of
these sounds?
It is a synthesizer.

The synthesizer is
an **electronic** instrument.
It looks like a small piano.
It has a computer inside of it.
This helps the synthesizer make
many different sounds.
It can sound like a drum, a trumpet,
a flute, or even a tuba!

Vocabulary

beaters—small sticks used to play percussion instruments. *Sally uses beaters to play her xylophone.*

bell—the wide, round part of a musical instrument from where sound comes. *The tuba has the widest bell of all the instruments.*

bow—a piece of wood with horsehairs stretched across it used to play stringed instruments. *The violinist moved the bow back and forth across the strings.*

crook—the curved metal tube that forms the mouthpiece of the bassoon. *The bassoonist put a new reed on the crook of his instrument.*

drumhead—material that is stretched over the top and bottom of a drum. *The drummer rapped on the drumhead with the drumsticks.*

electronic—using electricity and a computer to function. *Electronic instruments like the synthesizer must be plugged in.*

Keys—parts of a musical instrument that are pressed to make sounds. *A flute has many round keys.*

mouthpiece—a part of a musical instrument on which the mouth is placed. *Jean blew air into the mouthpiece of her saxophone.*

pegs—small pins found on the neck of musical instruments used to tighten, or tune, the strings. *The cello player turned the pegs on his instrument to tune it.*

reed—a small, specially shaped piece of wood that attaches to the mouthpiece of woodwind instruments. *Allison blew air over her clarinet's reed.*

valves—parts on brass instruments that are pressed to make sounds. *The trumpet player placed one finger over each of her instrument's three valves.*

Think About It!

1. What are the little knobs on a trumpet called?

2. Which instruments are part of the string family?

3. Why are percussion instruments important?

4. Which woodwind instrument does not have a reed?

5. What happens when a piano key is pressed?

The Story and You!

1. If you could play any musical instrument, which one would you choose? Why?

2. Think of three important things that you would need to learn in order to play a musical instrument.

3. Think of three ways that you could make a musical instrument at home.

4. Think of three places where you would see people playing musical instruments.

5. If a tuba could talk, what do you think it would say?